Wilbur, The <u>Really</u> Special Horse

By Tammy Kay Corbin

Cover illustration by
Jeanne Mellin

Author photograph by
Libby Rosen

ISBN-10: 1449509568
EAN-13: 9781449509569

Printed in the U.S.A.

*For my Lord and Savior,
Jesus Christ. Every word
in this book came from
Him.*

*In honor of Ann Eaton,
Wilbur's "mommy" and a
very special person in my
life.*

*In special memory of
my mother, mentor and
friend, June Graves.*

Table of Contents

Wilbur, The <u>Really</u> Special Horse

1.

MEET WILBUR

I would like you to meet my best friend, Wilbur. Now I know it would seem natural that my best friend would be a human being like myself— or at best, a dog. They say man's best friend is a dog. Well, my best friend is a horse!

He wasn't always my best friend. We met many years ago on a very cold, windy day. I had been invited to ride Wilbur to see if I might be able to help his owner sell him.

You see, he had been a Champion show horse and the trainer he had been living with had moved far away, so Wilbur came home to stay with his owner.

He had a very big pasture to stay in full of lush, green grass, and plenty of horse friends, and a nice big shelter he could go in for warmth on bad weather days.

Now, in Wilbur's mind, this was the life! It sure beat standing in a stall all day waiting for his turn to be exercised by the trainer, and then put back in his stall.

There was a time that Wilbur actually preferred the life of a Champion show horse. He enjoyed showing off his talent and being in front of whooping and hollering people. He knew they were all standing up and clapping for him!

He won pretty rosettes, ribbons, and trophies. He was even put in the spotlight several times to make a victory pass after all the other horses left the ring.

There was a lot of pressure in those days to succeed though. Wilbur always tried to be his best for his trainer, for he was quite fond of him.

One night Wilbur was not feeling quite well. His trainer didn't notice. The most important class of the show was ahead. This was what was on the trainer's mind.

As the trainer started into the show ring Wilbur refused to enter the ring. He just knew he was not going to be able to perform his best and didn't want to let his trainer down and disappoint him.

His trainer just thought Wilbur was being disobedient, so he tried correcting him with a whipping, but Wilbur still would not go.

Wilbur's relationship with his trainer was forever changed that day. Being a show horse wasn't fun any more.

Needless to say, when the trainer had to move far away and Wilbur was brought back to his owner's farm, Wilbur was happy, although a little scared about his future.

Four years had passed since Wilbur was brought home. Wilbur had not been ridden the entire time until the day I met him.

Of course, I did not know that Wilbur had any bad experiences at all. I just thought he was a Champion show horse needing to be reconditioned so his owners could sell him. They wanted him to find a new home and have a more useful life than standing in a pasture.

When I started to mount up to ride him, he tried his best to talk to me and tell me he did not want to be ridden again. He didn't want to feel all that pressure and take a chance on letting any humans down ever again. He stomped his feet and shook his head and shoved me with his nose.

I did not understand his horse language back then. I just thought he was a bit excited and hesitant because he hadn't been ridden for so long.

I actually took some video of that day, and now when I watch it, it seems so obvious to me!

How could I have missed his clear communication? He did not try to throw me off that day when I rode him, but he seemed very nervous.

I didn't take him home with me that day, as my two stalls were full and I had no place to put him, but he had found a place in my heart. I told his owners I would call them if I ever got a place to put him.

2.

WHO IS THIS HORSE?

Three more years passed before I was able to bring Wilbur to my house, and the events that happened those three years prior to his arrival is an entire story in itself, so I will not take the time right now to tell you!

The day I brought the horse trailer to take Wilbur to my home he was very nervous, scared, and downright angry. He had gotten used to the lush green pasture and his wonderful herd of horse friends. "Where exactly is this lady taking me, and what is she going to do to me?" he thought.

The first two weeks I spent just brushing him and loving him and doing some groundwork with him, as he was extremely fat from all that lush green grass, and was out of shape!

He got tired and sweaty really quick, so I would have to cool him out carefully so he wouldn't get sick.

The day finally came when I thought he was ready to ride safely. I had never quite experienced a horse like this. Something was wrong, but what?

He did not try to rear or buck or throw me off, but he was not acting right. He would stop, or turn (without being asked to turn), or start backing up.

Well, of course, a Champion show horse knows how to be ridden and does not act like this, so as a trainer person I thought he was being disobedient. I gave him a little smack with my riding crop. He immediately went down on the ground as if I had shot him with a gun.

Now I may not be the smartest person on earth, but I had enough common sense to know this was NOT a normal reaction by a normal horse. Exactly who WAS this horse, and exactly what issues made him act like this?

I had a talk with him that day and promised I would never strike him again, but instead, I would help him heal and get better.

There was a little additional problem though. How do you sell a horse that is not "normal" and cannot be ridden easily? I had to call his owners and break the news to them. This would not be a quick turn around. It may take me a while to get him re-trained and sold. I offered to buy him but his selling price was more money than I could afford.

3.

WILBUR BECOMES "WILBUR"

Every day now became a challenge. It was like reading a mystery that always had two different story lines going on at the same time, and you never knew what the next chapter would bring and how the mystery would unravel.

There were days I would work with Wilbur and he would just run into fences or trees, or just go down to his knees for no reason. I would always just talk to him and reassure him that everything was going to be all right and encourage him to move on.

I introduced him to children that come to my house to learn and ride. He seemed to sense the innocence of the children and knew they were not trainer-types that might hurt him. He started making a special bond with the children, especially the smaller ones.

This is when he let his true personality show, and when Wilbur became "Wilbur".

You see, when Wilbur was born he was given a very long, fancy name that was put on his Registration papers. Before I brought him to my house, I asked his owners if he had a nickname and they said he did not.

He had quite the raging appetite. When he first came to my house, I would have to take something in with me to protect myself every time I would put feed in his stall, as he would almost seem like an attack horse!

As he would eat, I would gently stroke his neck and talk calmly to him. I would tell him to settle down and not act that way.

The more I got to know this horse and the more I worked with him it became evident that there was a very gentle, kind, compassionate, loving soul inside that horse that was begging to be understood. He also wanted to understand and trust the humans around him again.

At my house, he freely roams the fenced five acres surrounding it, and has a stall to stay in as needed. When watching him play with the other horses I noticed he was always the one to be kind and understanding to the others- never mean or pushy.

He even learned not to be so rude at dinnertime. He totally reminded me of the sweet, gentle soul that Wilbur the pig displayed in the book, "Charlotte's Web".

I was sharing that thought with him one day and was teasing him that I should call him Wilbur. I expected he would not think much of being nicknamed after a pig.

From that day forward, when I called him in from the field I would call out "WILLLBUUR", similar to the way Mr. Ed would talk to his human owner (named Wilbur) in the famed show of the 1960's, "Mr. Ed". This nickname was always just between him and me at that point. I would never want to embarrass him.

4.

ONE STEP FORWARD, TWO STEPS BACK

Day after day, Wilbur and I worked together. He was full of fear and anger and needed to learn to let it all go.

He trusted the children more than he trusted me, and would let them ride him. He did not act quite like a "normal" horse, but he never ran into things or had a meltdown when the children would ride. He would try to do what he thought they wanted.

We would play tag on horseback as a group and the one day that Wilbur finally figured out what was going on he started to canter and go faster so he wouldn't be tagged "it". He scared his little girl half to death because she thought he was running away with her.

As soon as he sensed her fear he stopped dead in his tracks without her asking him to, and just about sent her flying over his head! Yes, this was the new Wilbur emerging.

He got a bit better about me riding him, but the key was NOT to put saddles and bridles on him when I rode, as this connected me to his brain as a "trainer-type". When I was riding him bareback without bits in his mouth he was able to see me as a friend he could trust. To be honest though, he always seemed to like it much better when I was on the ground and he could see me.

I even started to introduce a harness and cart to him again, as I knew he had won some of his past Championships at the horse shows pulling a cart. This did not go so well at first.

I had asked my daughter to help and used my training knowledge to go about this task professionally and safely, which included NOT doing it alone!

Well, running into walls while pulling a cart

is not something I consider very fun, OR safe!

Wilbur was just too scared and pressured to be

able to handle it.

Wilbur has taught me a lot about being non-

traditional. I went about his re-training to the

cart in a very non-traditional, non-safe way,

which included using only him, the cart and me.

I told him, "I will not feel you have your

head on straight enough to let me drive you until

you have it on straight enough to stand by

yourself with your harness on in the middle of the

arena, wait patiently while I get the cart out, pull

it up behind you, and hook up both sides by myself."

This took fewer days than I expected and before I knew it, I was in front, leading him around with the empty cart pulled behind him.

I eventually worked my way back and sat in the cart. He was starting to give me some fun drives.

As much as he seemed to like doing this with me and for me, something about him was changing. I could not put my finger on it. He seemed so tired. He was still eating all his food, but not with the same spark as I was used to seeing. He seemed depressed.

I thought he might be getting sick, so I would take his temperature and keep a watch on him. He never showed signs of illness, so I thought he might be utilizing extra energies in self-healing. He had been making such progress lately!

Then it happened. I went out to feed one Saturday morning and he was lying down and seemed to be totally drained of energy. He did not eat all his breakfast and he just wanted to rest. He still did not have a fever or any other symptoms.

I called his owners and said if he did not eat his dinner I would call the vet, which I did.

The vet came out the next day and got a blood sample to take to the lab to help diagnose him. Later that evening I was calling her again because he seemed to be feeling very poorly and I was worried about him.

The lab results showed an extremely high white blood count, which pointed to infection somewhere. Nothing in the lab results indicated a problem with kidneys or liver or anything else.

The vet decided we would put him on two different antibiotic injections daily to see if that would improve his condition.

I became trained to do injections..... me, who always had a fear of needles to the point it kept me from pursuing a much-desired career in nursing. I did not mind needles being put into me. I just did not want to be putting them into others!

Wilbur once again was so cooperative and helpful. He knew I had no idea what I was doing. Well, at least I was not comfortable doing what I had to do.

He let me put those big needles in his rear and never once offered to kick at me or object.

He knew I was trying to help him. He still did not have a fever. No symptoms at all, but being tired.

That afternoon he finally had a HUGE symptom. His breathing was extremely labored. On top of that, he finally had a fever.

I called the vet and his owners. We decided I would make the trip with him in the trailer to go to the Vet Hospital emergency room.

By the time I got there it was 9 p.m. I remember the exact date, February 3, 2006, and the fact that when we arrived he was breathing with his mouth open by then.

The emergency room staff went right to work, taking his vital signs. They did blood work and performed an ultrasound. The ultrasound gave us some answers. This poor horse had developed triple pneumonia. His lungs were full

of fluid (pneumonia). His chest cavity was full of

fluid outside his lungs (plural pneumonia). He

also had huge enclosed balls of infection in his

lungs (abscessing pneumonia).

When talking about this evening later, the vets

told me Wilbur was "a walking dead horse".

They put tubes into his lungs and drained

over three buckets of fluid out of his right lung

and over two buckets of fluid out of his left lung.

They did not give much hope of him pulling

through. They said the treatment necessary to try

to save him would be very, very expensive, as in

thousands of dollars.

I stood there with a revelation going through my head. I said a silent prayer and gave thanks to God that my offer to buy him previously had been denied. If I owned him, I would not have had the money to save his life.

I certainly did not expect his owners to spend thousands of dollars either. This horse was twelve years old (not extremely old for a horse, but getting beyond his peak in value), especially when he wasn't a "normal" horse and wasn't even given odds as good as 50-50 to survive.

Wilbur is blessed with owners that truly care about their horses, not because they are worth money, but because they are in their hearts and part of their family.

Wilbur had good days and bad days while in the Vet Hospital Intensive Care Unit. I would drive the forty-five minutes to see him every day... sometimes twice a day. I would take him treats and his favorite hay.

Strangely enough, my sister-in-law was in the hospital ICU around the corner during this same time, so I would often visit both of them.

Wilbur was in so much pain and really struggling for his life. I had to learn not to be selfish, but instead be willing to let him go. I had a talk with him one day and released him. I told him if he wanted to pass out of this life, that he didn't have to stay around on my account.

I had to learn to release my sister-in-law also. She passed away on February 19, 2006 at the young age of 46.

The next day, when lying down with Wilbur in his hospital stall he bit at me and was angry, as if to say "Don't you EVER give up on me. I don't appreciate that." I heard him loud and clear.

I arranged a visit for the children to go to the vet hospital to see Wilbur. It was a special day and meant a lot to him. We took pictures.

The vets said the only thing that he had going for him was his spirit and strong will to live. He spent 30 days in ICU. He was released to come back to my house March 3, 2006. By this time all the vets, vet students and my students were all calling him "Wilbur".

He was home, but he was not well yet. He spent nine months on three different types of antibiotics that he needed three times a day, and his vitals needed monitored several times a day as well.

We set him up a "horsey hospital wing" at my house. He had a separate barn, stall and paddock all to himself. He was not well enough to be with the others. We prayed over him daily, asking for God's grace and mercy and claimed a total healing of this horse.

Wilbur went back to the vet hospital in July 2006 for a recheck and ultrasound. Although his blood work showed improvement, his left lung still had some abscesses and fluid and his right lung was pretty much gone. It had started to become scar tissue and shrink.

The good news though, the vets said, was a horse could live with one lung and have a fairly normal life, just "not the life of a race horse."

I called Wilbur's owners and shared the news, but was privately surprised that he only had one lung. So many people had been praying over him and believing in a miracle. I cut my losses and thanked God that Wilbur was even alive.

We continued his health care at home and he continued to hold his own and cooperate with taking all his medicine. He was literally taking 124 human pills a day that we made into liquid form (laced with a little peppermint extract for taste) and put it down his mouth.

Needless to say, about six months into it he was really sick and tired of being sick and tired and taking all this medicine. Staying true to form, he would find the strength in himself to cooperate.

I made another trailer trip down to the vet hospital with him for a checkup in October 2006. I listened to the vets talk to each other as they were doing his ultrasound, "Normal lung, normal lung, some pockets of fluid here, but basically a normal lung."

Then they looked up at me and said, "Wait a minute. Isn't this his BAD side?"

"Yes," I said, with tears in my eyes.

"Well, this horse has a working lung on this side. Not 100%, but pretty good considering."

I could hardly wait to get to my truck and
call Wilbur's owners on my cell phone. Luckily,
they answered.

"Wilbur has TWO LUNGS," I said, out-and-
out crying at this point. I could not hold it back
any longer.

Praise God! What a testimony! What a
special horse.

5.

WHERE DO WE GO FROM HERE?

Eleven months from the time Wilbur got sick, I was given the go-ahead to start conditioning him again. I took it nice and slow. He seemed to have lost a lot of his confidence, and did not want to move if I was on his back and he couldn't see me. As he got better, I started to put some of the lighter children on his back.

He was fine as long as I was attached to him and he could see me. A long lunge line was not good enough. I had to be the one actually steering the reins.

I accomplished this by putting long lines (reins used for driving a horse- not riding) through the stirrups while a rider was on his back.

Once again, I was using a non-traditional (most likely not-safe) method, but it worked. Eventually Wilbur "graduated" and even learned to start jumping a little. He had a jumping part in our annual recital in October 2007. He was so proud and I was so proud of him!

6.

WILBUR, THE SLEDDING HORSE

There is something very human-like about Wilbur. I guess all horses can be human-like and communicate with us quite well in their own special way if we take the time to listen.

This mirrors how I feel about the Lord as well. He communicates with us *very* well when we stop and take the time to listen.

In the winter of Wilbur's recovery, once he graduated from his "hospital wing" at my house he was once again in the field with the others.

He would let the others go about their business and would give me moral support as I did the chores.

We don't have much land here, and no large tractor or manure spreader, so it is a daily activity for me to not only muck out all the stalls by hand, but also to carry it as far out as possible and spread it by hand as well.

I am a fairly small person, and if you don't already know it, let me tell you. Horse manure mixed with bedding is extremely bulky and heavy!

I have had to get very creative to keep my health! My first great idea was not to hand carry the equine muck buckets they sell at the stores, but instead to use a 32 gallon Rubbermaid trash can strapped to a handcart dolly and wheel it out. I found it much easier to pull than to push.

This worked fairly well when I had fewer horses and carried it not quite so far. In the muddy season the wheels would get stuck and made it very difficult though.

When winter came and the snow was deep, it was next to impossible to get the dolly to move at all. Through sheer determination and knowledge that "I can do all things through Christ, who strengthens me" (Philippians 4:13), we worked as a team, the Lord and I, and load after load, kept getting them dumped and spread.

One day a sled caught my eye that was in the corner of our garage. The sled had been purchased about the same time our three daughters were too old to care! The sled had been used only a couple times and it was an especially large one, big enough to hold two or three people.

"Hmmmm... wonder how that would work in place of my handcart dolly?" I thought. I tried it, and it was absolutely wonderful.

The sled went over the snow with ease, pulling two muck buckets a trip. I had a whole new life!

As the snow became mud, and the sled got harder to pull, Wilbur would stand in the area I dumped in and just stare at me with his big, kind eyes, as if to say, "Why don't you let me help you? I helped create this mess. I can help clean it up."

"Right, Wilbur! You can hardly breathe and are still too scared to pull a cart again. I'm sure you'd do a great job pulling this sled for me," and I would just go about my business. Remember, this was in 2006 as he was still recovering.

A year later, I'm finding myself in the same position. The mud is just overbearing. I have nine horses now and it is all I can do to keep up with the workload.

There is dear Wilbur standing on the last pile of the previous eleven trips I made that day, looking at me and **begging** me to let him help. He is actually following me around, and will not leave me alone.

"Okay. Fine, Wilbur. You think you can do this. Let's go find out what we can work out," I could not believe what I heard myself saying.

I took him into the arena we built the past spring and put the harness on him we use to pull a cart.

Well, it took me about thirty minutes and three different ideas before I rigged up something I thought was halfway safe. I did not want him getting his back legs caught in the pull rope of the sled.

I decided not to use blinders (blinders are used to keep a horse from seeing what is behind them or beside them) or even a bit and bridle. I chose instead to use a halter and lead strap.

We started with a few baby steps forward at a walk. He seemed to be fine with it. I added a couple empty muck buckets and led him around the arena, doing turns, stopping, etc. He seemed totally overjoyed and somewhat relaxed.

"Okay Wilbur. We're ready for the big time." I opened the arena sliding doors, put two full muck buckets on the sled and off we went! He was so proud of himself and I felt so relieved at how physically undemanding this was for me. I praised him, and hugged him and thanked him. What a wonderful horse! We made an awesome team, Wilbur, the Lord and me.

7.

A HORSE IS ALWAYS A HORSE

Wilbur got so relaxed about pulling the muck buckets and sled for me! He would let me just hang the lead strap over his neck, dump one muck bucket, then dump another. Then I would get his lead and walk with him to go get another load. I never had anybody there to help me or hold him.

I would line the twelve full muck buckets up in a row and we would take two at a time. It was quite an ordeal to rig him up in the harness, so we would consolidate and do this just once a day.

One evening <u>much</u> past dark, we were doing our dumping ritual. There was actually snow on the ground so I should have been dumping on my own without Wilbur's help. He had gotten me so spoiled rotten it never crossed my mind to not have his help!

We were working using the floodlights to light our path, and had dumped five loads and were on our last load of the day. I dumped one muck bucket and as I turned around to put it on the sled and get the other one, something startled Wilbur.

No sooner than he moved and I said "whoa", he was off at a full run, sled and all, before I could grab the lead strap off his neck.

Once he was scared he lost his human qualities and became a true horse... a prey animal that takes flight in the wild to survive. He thought that scary object running behind him was out to eat him alive, and he was running for his life.

I felt a total sickness in my stomach and panic come over me, but I heard the words in my head I have often said to others. "Don't panic. Stay calm and act calm and trust in God."

Wilbur was running for the electric fence and I knew he was in trouble. I have heard terror stories of electric fencing cutting right through a horse's leg or chest, and he was running full speed ahead, right for it.

It is dark and hard to see, but I can see him run right into the fence and bounce back off it and keep running, still dragging the sled behind him.

I hear God telling me, "Call him. Wilbur trusts you and will come to you for safety." I start using the loudest, calmest voice I can muster, and start calling "WILLLBBUUUURRR.... WHOA WILLBBUUURRR. COME HERE WILLLBBBBUUUUURR."

I see him galloping right at me, and for a split second, I see my life pass right before me, and know I am going to die. "He's going to run right over me," I am thinking. And I thank God for all the blessings He has given me and even for this crazy horse who is about to kill me, and I ask God to save the horse and take care of the entire herd for me, and I praise Him again and thank Him for doing so.

It is amazing the speed thoughts can run through your head when they don't have much time to! By now Wilbur is running right past me, so close I could have reached out and touched him, but so fast that I couldn't.

He was running for the arena. Sled, harness and all still attached. I ran as fast as I could to close the arena doors behind him, because I knew he could only run so far and fast in there. It was a much safer environment, and it had LIGHTS!

I am praying the whole time I am running that God will spare this horse's life, because I know I am going to see life-threatening injuries... most likely an open gash in his chest and/or front legs.

It did not take long for him to stop once he was in the arena and he saw me. He was steaming hot and breathing ever so hard. I did not see any blood, except a small mark on his back left leg.

I got the sled off and hugged him and told him how very sorry I was that I put him in a position to possibly kill himself. I forgot he was a horse, and that a horse is ALWAYS a horse, and can react unreliably at any time, because God created them as prey animals. I had turned him into my human-like partner and totally forgot about the prey animal side.

I told Wilbur, "After I get you cooled down, we have to revisit this entire incident. You have come much too far in your healing to be traumatized by this the rest of your life."

The forty-five minute plan to dump the muck buckets turned into a three-hour journey. I got him cooled down, doctored up his leg, then realized his breathing had returned to normal pretty quick. "His lungs must not be in too bad of shape," I thought.

I hooked him back up to the sled. As you can imagine, he wasn't quite the willing partner I had before. We did baby steps around the arena pulling the sled, but his eyes were about to bulge out of his head in fear. He did it for me though because I asked him to.

"Now we have to go outside Wilbur. Not a smart move, because you are much stronger than I am, and with fear added to that equation, I'm not sure I can keep you under control, but we've GOT to do it. I'm going to trust you in that you'll trust me, and we're going to do this together, with God's help."

I was praying the entire trip outside, as I knew this could be a total disaster, and I was trusting in God the way I was asking Wilbur to trust in me. Believe me, it was by the grace of God we completed that trip, because Wilbur was shaking and scared to death, and so was I.

We came to a certain turn to change direction and the floodlights made our shadows appear as if we were giants, and he got even more scared. I believe that is what spooked him, or maybe the floodlights reminded him somehow of the spotlights in his earlier years and he mentally snapped before he physically spooked. I cannot be sure.

When I was putting him to bed that night I apologized to him again, as I could hear him apologizing to me. He felt he let me down.

I assured him it was the other way around and that I would never let him down and put him in that position again. I also dropped to my knees in prayer and thanked God for saving this horse's life.

"Wilbur," I said. "You must be a really special horse. God has chosen to save your life twice now. He must have some really special things in store for you."

At that very moment, I heard that quiet whisper that I have come to recognize as my Lord and Savior. "You are to write a book to share this special horse and his testimony with others."

I hate to admit it, but sometimes I am a smart aleck with God. I talked back to him, my voice quite stern. "You have got to be kidding me! You mean to tell me that you scared me to death and put me through all these emotions and panic so I could write a book?"

"No." I hear. "I'm here to tell you that I can take even the worse situations and turn them into something good. You made an honest mistake and I will honor you as you have honored me, and use it for my good."

"Thank you Lord. I am humbled. Thank you for giving me your strengths in place of my weaknesses. Thank you for your constant forgiveness, grace, mercy, guidance and wisdom. What an awesome God you are!"

I wonder where the next chapter in Wilbur's life will lead me, and how God will use us both. I can hardly wait to find out!